AWESOME FORCES OF NATURE

HOWLING HURRICANES

Revised and Updated

Louise and Richard Spilsbury

Heinemann
LIBRARY

Chicago, Illinois

www.heinemannraintree.com
Visit our website to find out
more information about
Heinemann-Raintree books.

To order:

☎ Phone 888-454-2279

🖥 Visit www.heinemannraintree.com
to browse our catalog and order online.

©2004, 2010 Heinemann Library
an imprint of Capstone Global Library, LLC
Chicago, Illinois

13 12 11 10
10 9 8 7 6 5 4 3 2 1

Edited by Megan Cotugno, Abby Colich, and Andrew Farrow
Designed by Richard Parker
Original illustrations © Capstone Global Library 2004
Illustrated by Geoff Ward
Picture research by Hannah Taylor
Production by Alison Parsons
Originated by Capstone Global Library, Ltd.
Printed and bound in China by Leo Paper Products, Ltd.

Library of Congress Cataloging-in-Publication Data

Spilsbury, Louise.
  Howling hurricanes / Louise and Richard Spilsbury.
    p. cm.
  Includes bibliographical references and index.
  ISBN 978-1-4329-3781-2 (hc) -- ISBN 978-1-4329-3788-1
(pb) 1. Hurricanes--Juvenile literature. I. Spilsbury, Richard,
1963- II. Title.
  QC944.2.S725 2010
  551.55'2--dc22
                          2009037483

Acknowledgments
We would like to thank the following for permission to
reproduce photographs: Art Directors & Trip: 4 (Viesti
Collection); Capstone Publishers: 26 (Karon Dubke); Corbis: 5
(EPA/Smiley N. Pool), 10 (Reuters), 13 (Dallas Morning News/
Smiley N. Pool), 16 (EPA/Piyal Adhikary); Getty Images: 14
(Mario Villafuerte), 21 (Chris Graythen); NOAA: 8, 25; Panos:
6 (Bruce Paton); Photolibrary: 19 (Index Stock Imagery),
24 (Javier Larrea); Press Association: 20 (AP Photo/John
McConnico), 23 (AP Photo/Victor Caivano), 28 (AP Photo);
Reuters: 9, 15; Rex Features: 17 (Sipa Press), 27 (Sipa Press);
Science Photo Library: 7, 18 (Nasa-Goddard Space Flight
Centre); Still Pictures: 22 (Julio Etchart).

Cover photograph of Hurricane Wilma approaching Cancun,
Mexico in 2005 reproduced with permission of Reuters (Daniel
Aguilar).

We would like to thank Dr. Ramesh Srivastava for his
invaluable help in the preparation of this book.

Contents

Any words appearing in the text in bold, **like this**, are explained in the glossary.

What Is a Hurricane?

Hurricanes are the most powerful storms on Earth. They grow from **tropical** storms over the sea. Some stay over the open ocean, far from land, and some weaken and die out before they reach land. Others hurtle toward a shore at high speed.

Hurricane winds often travel at speeds of over 300 kilometers (186 miles) per hour—faster than many of the fastest trains! If hurricanes reach land, their violent, fast winds and heavy rain can cause terrible damage and destruction. Some only last for days. Others can go on for weeks. Hurricanes usually cause most damage around coasts, but big hurricanes can sometimes reach far inland.

These waves are being whipped up by a Caribbean hurricane. The word "hurricane" is said to come from the name of a god of evil, "Hurican." People in the Caribbean in the past gave it this name because of its destructive power.

This is some of the massive damage to Gilchrist, Texas. It was caused by Hurricane Ike in September 2008.

Hurricanes cause great destruction when they move onto land. They can blow down buildings, pull up trees, and throw cars and boats around like toys. They can whip up the sea to form giant waves that crash onto shores. The strong winds also push massive quantities of water on shore. This is called a **storm surge**. Heavy rains and storm surges can cause floods when land that is normally dry is covered in water. In the past, hurricanes killed many people. Today, **scientists** usually spot dangerous hurricanes early and warn people to move to a safe place.

Top hurricane speeds

No one really knows exactly how fast the fastest hurricanes go because measuring equipment is often destroyed by the hurricane. Some scientists believe that the fastest hurricane winds are around 300 kilometers (186 miles) an hour, while others say they might reach 600 kilometers (372 miles) per hour!

How Do Hurricanes Happen?

Hurricanes always begin over warm water. Warm water heats the air just above it and supplies water vapor to it. Water vapor is water in the form of a gas. The warm, moist air is lighter and it rises. As it rises, the water vapor turns back into liquid water to form clouds. When the layer of warm air moves up, cooler air fills the space it has left. This movement causes winds.

Over **tropical** waters that reach very high temperatures, the heat makes the air rise very quickly. As the winds and clouds rise, they move faster and faster. They also start to **rotate** in a spiral. When the winds in this spinning storm reach about 120 kilometers (74 miles) per hour, it is called a hurricane. The whirling pattern of the winds makes the air inside the hurricane move even faster.

Hurricanes may begin like this—as winds that merely whip up waves on the sea. A hurricane usually takes days to develop. The fastest a hurricane might form is two days.

How do hurricanes die?

Hurricanes are created and powered by the heat and water vapor that comes off very warm water. As hurricanes move over land or over cooler parts of the ocean, the supply of water vapor is reduced or cut off and they weaken and start to die out. A hurricane without warm water is like a toy car with a rundown battery—it gradually loses power and then stops altogether.

If fast enough, winds above a warm sea can start spinning within 12 hours. You can see the winds spiraling fast in this picture from above a hurricane, taken from a space shuttle.

Naming hurricanes

Scientists give hurricanes actual names. They do this so that everyone who talks about a particular hurricane, whether they are scientists or ordinary people, know which one it is. The names go in alphabetical order. For Atlantic hurricanes, scientists don't use Q, U, X, Y or Z as there are few names starting with these letters.

What is a hurricane's eye?

The **eye** of a hurricane is at its center, inside the swirling mass of wind and cloud. If you could fly high above a hurricane and look down inside it, it would look like water spinning around a drain. The center is calm and the strongest winds spin around it in the **eyewall**. When the eye passes over land, people below feel just a gentle breeze and the rain stops. As the hurricane moves on, the winds at the edge of the eye—the eyewall—begin again.

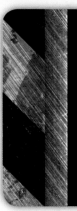

Making a mini-hurricane eye

You can create your own mini-hurricane eye after a bath. When the water spirals around the drain, right in the middle there is a dry center. This is just like the eye of a hurricane, except that in a hurricane you get huge spiraling winds and clouds instead of swirling water.

This is a **satellite** image of Hurricane Katrina. Can you see the eye of the hurricane? Most hurricanes have an eye between 30 and 60 kilometers (18 and 37 miles) across.

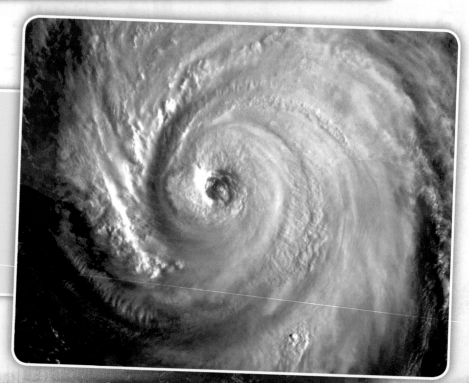

How do hurricane rains form?

Hurricanes almost always bring very heavy rains. This is because they pick up water vapor as they travel across warm waters. They do this by a process called **evaporation**. The process of evaporation turns liquid water into a gas called water vapor. Evaporation increases rapidly as the liquid water becomes warmer. This is how wet clothes dry outside after washing. The water inside them is warmed by the air and evaporates, leaving the clothes dry.

Water vapor turns back into liquid water when it cools. This is the reverse of evaporation, called **condensation**. In a hurricane, the air cools as it rises. The water vapor then condenses into liquid water and falls out as rain.

Large hurricanes can carry vast amounts of water vapor. This means that they can cause incredibly heavy rainstorms, like this one during Hurricane Keith, which hit Belize in October 2000.

Where Do Hurricanes Happen?

Hurricanes only start over really warm water, so they only form in certain parts of the world. Hurricanes never start over cold oceans, such as the South Atlantic. They form over **tropical** oceans. These areas of water are near the **equator**, an imaginary line around the center of the Earth, where it is always very warm.

When is a hurricane not a hurricane?

Hurricanes are called different names in different parts of the world. These storms are called hurricanes when they happen over the North Atlantic and Northeast Pacific oceans. When they occur in the Pacific and Indian Oceans, they are called typhoons or cyclones. Even though they have different names, they are the same kind of storm.

This woman stands among the debris caused by Cyclone Nargis. It hit Burma (Myanmar) in May 2008, causing over 145,000 deaths and massive destruction.

Hurricanes on the move

Once a storm has started, it does not stay in one place. Hurricanes can travel thousands of kilometers over the oceans. They move like a spinning top—spiraling around their **eye** at high speeds. At the same time, the whole storm moves slowly forward or backward in another direction. Most hurricanes travel generally west or northward. The average speed for a hurricane to travel is 10 kilometers (6 miles) an hour.

Hurricanes occur in the **northern hemisphere** and cyclones happen mostly in the **southern hemisphere**. Hurricanes and cyclones usually spin in opposite directions. This is because the Earth is turning slowly all the time. As it turns, the winds blowing above Earth's surface are pulled in different directions. The Earth's rotation causes the spin to be clockwise in the northern hemisphere and counterclockwise in the southern hemisphere.

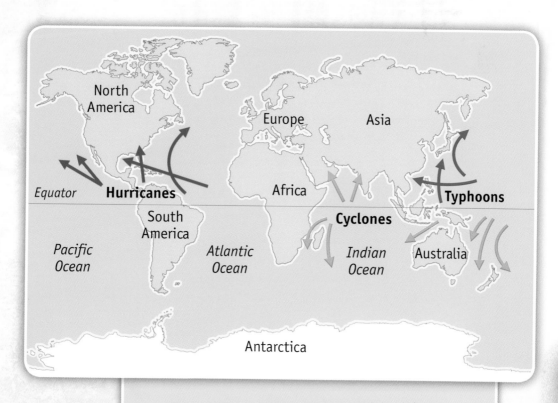

The arrows on this world map show where hurricanes, cyclones, and typhoons usually form and the routes that they usually take.

When do hurricanes happen?

Hurricanes happen every year. There has been a hurricane, cyclone, or typhoon recorded every year for the past 500 years. It is likely that they happened just as regularly before that, too. Every year there is also at least one major hurricane that reaches land somewhere and causes damage or destruction.

Hurricanes always happen at certain times of the year, known as the **hurricane seasons**. In **tropical** oceans and seas, like the Gulf of Mexico and the Caribbean Sea, the hurricane season begins in May or June. In the Atlantic Ocean the season runs from June 1 to November 30. Hurricane seasons may last up to six months, but the worst storms usually happen over a two-month period—for example, August and September in the northeastern Pacific.

This graph shows the number of hurricanes that have happened at certain times of year over the past century in the Atlantic Ocean, the Caribbean Sea, and the Gulf of Mexico. As you can see, the peak of the hurricane season is from mid-August to late October.

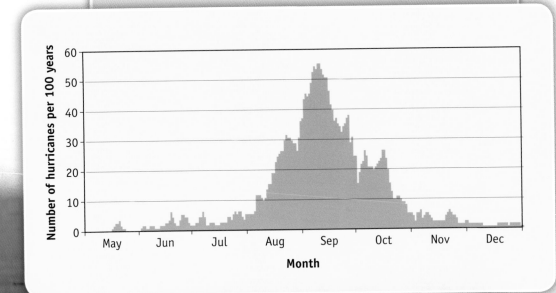

Hurricane Katrina, 2005

Hurricane Katrina hit the gulf coast of the United States on August 28, 2005. It was one of the deadliest and costliest hurricanes in United States history. Although many areas were affected, most damage occurred to the city of New Orleans, Louisiana. The city was built on low-lying land and protected by **levees**. The hurricane's **storm surge** pushed water over and through the levees, flooding the city. Officials had asked people to **evacuate**, but many stayed. Afterward, government response and rescue efforts were disorganized. It was difficult to help the people in need.

> " *It's like being in a third world country. We're trying to work without power. Everyone knows we're all in this together. We're just trying to stay alive.*
>
> —Mitch Handrich, a registered nurse manager at Charity Hospital in New Orleans "

Water covers homes just east of downtown New Orleans. Many residents of the area were displaced after the disaster and forced to move elsewhere.

13

What Happens in a Hurricane?

As a hurricane passes directly over people or places, there are three different stages. First, wind builds up, becoming very fast and bringing heavy rain. Then the wind dies down and the rain stops. This is when the calm center—the **eye**—of the hurricane passes over. This can last for minutes or even hours, as hurricanes sometimes hover over one place. Then, it moves on and the other side of the hurricane passes over, bringing more fierce winds from the opposite direction and rain.

Hurricanes bring heavy showers of rain. These can cause flooding on land. A hurricane's high winds can whip up high waves that crash onto shores. Hurricanes can also cause **tornadoes**.

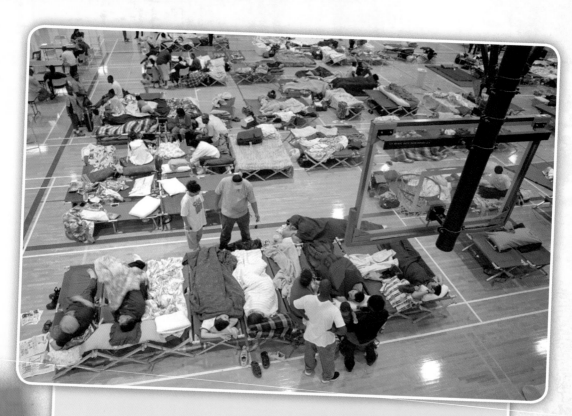

Many people have died after going outside while the eye of the storm was passing over, because they thought the hurricane was over. To be safe, people should stay in shelters like this one until the storm is completely over.

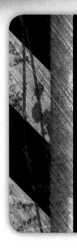

Tornadoes

Tornadoes can form in thunderstorms and hurricanes. A tornado is a tall funnel of wind that spins very fast. Tornadoes look like a rope of cloud coming down from a storm cloud. They are smaller and even faster than hurricane winds. Unlike hurricanes, tornadoes can travel far across land. This means they pass over more places where people live, causing a lot of damage.

What damage do hurricane winds cause?

Hurricane winds are so fast and strong they can move large objects as easily as blowing a hat off your head. Even the weakest hurricane winds can blow tiles off roofs, rattle windows, and snap branches. The worst hurricanes can blow down trees and move cars and **mobile homes**.

Strong hurricane winds often knock down electricity and telephone cables. This means people cannot use electric lights or stoves and may not be able to call others for help.

Rain damage

Hurricanes can drop huge amounts of rain over a short period of time. A big hurricane can drop so much rain that it causes floods. Floods are when land that is usually dry becomes covered with water. This can happen when rainwater makes rivers so high that the water spills over the sides and onto the land around it.

When floodwater sweeps through a town or city it can damage buildings and bury houses under mud. It drowns people if they cannot get away in time. When floodwater covers fields of **crops**, it ruins them and it can also drown farm animals. When this happens it can leave people dangerously short of food.

In 1996 Hurricane Fran dropped huge amounts of rain in Alexandria, Virginia. This heavy rainfall caused serious floods across the region.

What is a storm surge?

When a hurricane gets close to land, the winds can push a high wall of water in front of them. This is called a **storm surge**. When this kind of wave hits land, it can cause terrible damage to the coastline.

Storm surges can change the whole shape of the land. They may destroy beaches by dragging the sand and rocks out to sea. Sometimes they dump sand and create new beaches. Storm surges can also cover land and cause floods.

HURRICANE FACTS

These are things that people should do in a hurricane:

1 Stay indoors and keep away from windows.

2 If electricity is cut off, use flashlights to see in the dark. Do not use candles, which can cause fires if they are blown over.

3 Listen to radio or TV reports and take the advice given by experts and emergency services.

The combination of winds, rain, and storm surges causes terrible damage. In 1996 Hurricane Fran ruined thousands of homes and flattened millions of trees up to 240 kilometers (149 miles) inland from the sea in North Carolina.

CASE STUDY

Hurricane Andrew, 1992

The first hurricane in the **hurricane season** of 1992 arrived in southern Florida on August 24. It was named Hurricane Andrew. Hurricane Andrew's winds were spiraling at about 280 kilometers (174 miles) per hour. It traveled across land at about 30 kilometers (18 miles) per hour. As it moved over the warm waters of the Gulf of Mexico, it gained strength. It only began to weaken as it traveled over land across Louisiana. Hurricane Andrew caused over 60 deaths and huge amounts of damage.

> " *I've lived through ten hurricanes in my lifetime, and this is going to be the worst. I'm scared. I won't lie to you. I am scared.*
>
> —Louisiana café worker, Janice Semien "

This picture, taken over a period of four days, shows the movements of Hurricane Andrew between August 23 and 26, 1992.

What damage did Hurricane Andrew cause?

Andrew turned out to be one of America's most expensive hurricanes. Out at sea it churned up high waves, which toppled **oil platforms** and badly damaged **oil wells**. When it passed over coastlines, **storm surges** smashed millions of dollars' worth of boats and ships moored in the water.

The buildings and many other structures that Hurricane Andrew damaged or destroyed cost over $20 billion to repair or rebuild.

Scientists who were following the movements of the hurricane were able to warn people it was coming. About 2 million people were **evacuated**— they left their homes to stay somewhere safer. The hurricane damaged or destroyed houses, **mobile homes**, businesses, bridges, and roads. It also badly damaged the Louisiana fishing industry. Over 184 million fish were killed in one area alone!

Who Helps After a Hurricane?

After a hurricane has passed over, the danger does not end. Most people who die because of a hurricane drown in floods. Emergency service workers, such as fire rescue workers and the **armed forces**, get people to a safe place.

Other workers, from local hospitals and **aid organizations** like the Red Cross, set up first-aid stations to treat wounds. They also set up shelters where people who have been **evacuated** from their homes can stay. They give **evacuees** blankets, water, food, and any medical supplies they need. Emergency workers travel around the area to fix fallen electric power lines that could **electrocute** people and cut down damaged trees that could fall on them.

Sometimes rescue workers have to lift people out of dangerous fast-flowing flood water caused by hurricanes. This child was rescued from floods caused by Hurricane Hortense in Puerto Rico in September 1996.

Rich and poor

It takes time to put things back to normal after a hurricane. Bridges and buildings have to be rebuilt or repaired. Water companies fix broken **sewage** and water pipes. Government workers clean roads of obstructions such as mud, broken branches, and wrecked signs. Generally, people in rich, **developed countries** recover fairly quickly.

In a **developing country**, flooding from a hurricane can cause more long-term suffering. Poorer families usually do not have **insurance** or savings to pay for repairs. If their **crops** are ruined, they may starve. Aid organizations, such as Oxfam, and the governments of other countries send help. They may supply farm equipment, seeds, and farm animals. They may also send building equipment, so that people can rebuild their homes themselves.

Local residents in Pasadena, Texas, receive government **aid** after Hurricane Ike in September 2008.

Hurricane Mitch, 1998

In October 1998, a terrible hurricane raged across Central America. Winds up to 250 kilometers (155 miles) per hour swept through, bringing torrential rains up to 46 centimeters (18 inches) in one day. Hurricane Mitch left over 9,000 people dead, many missing, and millions more without homes. Roads and bridges were wrecked. Floods ruined farmland, **crops**, and people's food stores. Heavy rains caused **landslides**, too. A landslide is when mud and rock slide down a hill causing damage.

> 66
> *Some neighborhoods were flooded by water up to 1.5 meters (5 feet) high. People screamed asking for help and some of us, helped by tire inner tubes, threw ourselves in [the water] to rescue those trapped in their homes.*
>
> —Roberto Ramos, a Honduran nurse
> 99

KEY
— Mitch

Many people in Central America work on banana plantations (farms) like this. Hurricane Mitch destroyed most of the country's banana plants. This meant that many people lost their jobs and their chance of earning money to look after their families.

Long-term support

At first, **aid organizations** such as Oxfam and the Red Cross helped by giving people food, water, medical treatment, and somewhere to stay. They also helped people find family members who got lost in all the chaos.

Later their main aim was to get farms working again. That way people could feed themselves, without having to rely on help from other people. Aid organizations worked with local groups to plan what to do. Gradually, they helped people grow new corn, rice, bean, and banana plants to eat and sell. The poorest people in the area were the worst affected. Their houses were flimsy and had been completely wrecked by the hurricane. Aid organizations helped people build new, stronger homes, as well as new wells, bridges, and roads.

Many banana plantations had to be replanted with baby banana plants after the entire crop was destroyed by Hurricane Mitch in October 1998.

Can Hurricanes Be Predicted?

Predicting hurricanes is difficult because each one grows and moves differently. Some countries spend a lot of money on **scientists** and equipment to try to work out when and where hurricanes might happen. If they can work out where a hurricane is heading, they can tell people in that area to **evacuate**.

Satellite pictures

Weather **satellites** are special computers that are sent out into space. From space they photograph the clouds high above the Earth. This helps scientists on Earth to predict the weather. Hurricane experts study these pictures to see if there are any clouds that look like they could become hurricanes. They also use powerful supercomputers. These examine weather and hurricane information from around the world to help them with their predictions.

A scientist in Spain uses a computer linked to a weather satellite to view images of hurricanes. Predicting these huge storms is difficult, but new technology is continuing to make accuracy possible.

Hurricane hunters

When dangerous-looking storm clouds are spotted, hurricane hunters go to look at them. These people fly planes all around and into storms and hurricanes. They have special equipment to take measurements and pictures of the weather inside the storm.

For example, they drop miniature weather stations into a hurricane's **eyewall** on a parachute. This measures things like temperature, **humidity**, and wind speed. It sends the information to experts' computers. The experts look at this information along with satellite pictures and facts about the way that hurricanes in the past grew. This helps them to work out how strong a hurricane is and which way it is likely to go.

This is a National Oceanic and Atmospheric Administration (NOAA) operated Gulfstream IV-SP. The primary purpose of this jet is to assist in hurricane surveillance.

Can People Prepare for Hurricanes?

When **scientists** predict a hurricane, they send out warnings on TV and radio. If it is a very dangerous hurricane, this gives people time to **evacuate**. If it is a weaker hurricane, this gives people time to prepare for the storm. Most people who live in areas where there is a danger of hurricanes make some preparations in advance.

Long-term preparations

People can do several things to make their houses safer. For example, they can fix strong shutters to their windows. When these are closed, they stop hurricane winds shattering the glass. People also cut down dead branches or trees. During hurricanes these can cause a lot of damage when they snap off and blow about.

These are some essentials in an emergency disaster relief kit. Before **hurricane season**, governments tell people to stock up on supplies.

All animals must be kept safe as well, before and during a hurricane. People should take pets with them to their local shelter or evacuation area.

Governments can prepare for hurricanes further ahead, when planning new structures such as buildings and bridges. They can make stronger buildings that can cope with strong winds and rain. They can put important buildings, such as hospitals, further inland where they are safer from hurricanes. They can also build bigger storm drains that allow large amounts of water to soak away. This means that future floods will not be so deep.

HURRICANE FACTS

If a hurricane is on its way, but not one strong enough that people need to evacuate, there are still a number of steps that they should take:

1 People should check that their portable radio has batteries.

2 They should bring in or tie down loose objects outside, such as garden furniture.

3 They should close windows and shutters.

4 They should move food and other supplies into the basement or cellar (or the lowest room of the house) where people will be during the storm.

27

Can Hurricanes Be Prevented?

People have tried to prevent hurricanes in the past. In 1947 **scientists** tried to weaken a hurricane over water near America. They flew planes into the storm and dropped dry ice into the clouds to try to cool and calm it before it reached the shore. It did not work! Scientists today are working on new ideas, but we may never be able to stop hurricanes.

Scientists have learned a great deal about how hurricanes work. This is important, especially when more and more people are building homes near coastlines. Although it is impossible to predict all hurricanes, tracking and warning systems can help to save lives. They give people time to escape and lessen the damage these awesome forces of nature can cause.

In 1935 a hurricane hit the Florida Keys, killing around 408 people. In 1960 Hurricane Donna (right) hit the same area. Even though many more people were living there, early warnings meant that only three people died this time.

Howling Hurricanes of the Past

Galveston Hurricane, 1900
Storm-surge waves 4.5 meters (15 feet) high swamped the whole of Galveston and parts of the Texas coast. Around 8,000 people died.

Great Miami Hurricane, 1926
This storm caused over $100 million of damage in Florida. If the same storm were to happen today, it would cause over $80 billion of damage because there are so many more people living in Florida now!

Great Atlantic Hurricane, 1944
Over 20 centimeters (8 inches) of rain and 200-kilometer- (120-mile-) per hour winds caused 46 deaths on land and even more at sea.

Hurricane Camille, 1969
Huge floods struck after as much as 70 centimeters (8 inches) of rain fell in 5 hours when this hurricane hit the Mississippi Gulf Coast, killing over 250 people.

Cyclone Tracy, 1974
This hurricane hit Darwin, Australia, on Christmas morning, 1974. A total of 65 people were killed and 112 more were seriously injured. Around 80 percent of Darwin's homes were destroyed.

Hurricane David, 1979
This hurricane caused over $1 billion of damage to Dominica and the Dominican Republic in the Caribbean. Over 2,000 people were killed.

Typhoon Ike, 1984
Over a million people became homeless after Typhoon Ike hit the Philippines.

Hurricane Ike, 2008
Hurricane Ike was the largest known hurricane, measuring 1,000 kilometers (621 miles) wide. It devastated Central America and the United States Gulf Coast region.

Cyclone Nargis, 2008
This deadly cyclone hit Burma (Myanmar) in May 2008. Over 145,000 people were killed and massive destruction was caused.

Glossary

aid help given as money, medicine, food, or other essential items

aid organizations groups that raise money and provide help for people in need

armed forces army, air force, and navy. These forces have equipment to fight with, but also help rescue people at times.

condensation when water vapor turns into liquid water

crops plants grown to eat and to sell, such as rice and bananas

developed countries richer countries of the world that have well-developed services for their people, such as good hospitals and emergency services

developing countries poorer countries of the world that are gradually developing better conditions for their people

electrocute injure or kill with electricity

equator imaginary line around the center of the Earth

evacuate when people move from a dangerous place to somewhere safe

evacuee someone who moves from a dangerous place to somewhere safe

evaporate when water turns from liquid into a vapor (a gas in the air)

eye calm center of a hurricane

eyewall edge of the eye of a hurricane

humidity when the weather is very warm and moist at the same time

hurricane season some areas have hurricanes every year at about the same time. This is called the hurricane season.

insurance when people pay money regularly to a company that pays the full cost of rebuilding their home or business if it is damaged or destroyed

landslides when heavy rains and wind make large amounts of mud and rock slide down a hill or mountain

levees raised walls or banks at the edge of a river

mobile home home that can be moved

northern hemisphere everywhere on the Earth north of the equator

oil platform/well an oil platform is a building at sea around an oil well. An oil well is a deep narrow hole drilled to release oil found underground.

rotate spin or turn around

satellite object in space that sends out TV signals or takes photographs

scientists people who study aspects of the world around us

sewage waste matter from toilets and drains carried in sewers

southern hemisphere everywhere on the Earth south of the equator

storm surge when the sea becomes high along a coast due to storm winds

tornadoes fast-moving, spinning column of air that moves over land

tropical in the tropics—regions around the equator that have hot and humid weather

Find out more

Books

Langley, Andrew. *Hurricanes, Tsunamis, and Other Natural Disasters*. (New York: Kingfisher, 2006).

Oxlade, Chris. *Violent Skies: Hurricanes*. (Chicago: Raintree, 2005).

Pietras, Jamie. *Hurricane Katrina*. (New York: Chelsea House, 2008).

Websites

FEMA for Kids
www.fema.gov/kids/hurr.htm
For facts about hurricane dangers, what to do, quizzes, and more.

NASA Tropical Twisters
kids.earth.nasa.gov/archive/hurricane/index.html
Go right inside the eye of a hurricane with the hurricane hunters!

National Hurricane Center
www.nhc.noaa.gov
Read about the national hurricane center if you want to know more about tracking hurricanes.

Weather Wiz Kids
www.weatherwizkids.com/hurricane1.htm
Learn about hurricanes and lots of other weather patterns at this fun website.

Index